NOT DANCING

Books by Stephen Dunn

Looking for Holes in the Ceiling
Full of Lust and Good Usage
A Circus of Needs
Work and Love
Not Dancing

Not Dancing

Stephen Dunn

Carnegie-Mellon University Press
Pittsburgh 1984
Feffer and Simons, Inc., London

ACKNOWLEDGMENTS

American Poetry Review: "Sick Days," "The Room And the World"; *The American Scholar:* "Response To A Letter From France"; *Antaeus:* "In Defense of Blowfish," "Choosing To Live With It"; *Chelsea:* "Silence"; *Columbia Magazine:* "Traveling to Nova Scotia"; *The Georgia Review:* "The Dinner," "Enough Time"; *Kansas Quarterly:* "Blues For Another Time"; *The Missouri Review:* "Middle Class Poem," "An Argument With Wisdom At Montauk"; *New England Review:* "Kansas," "Atlantic City," "Briefcases," Reprinted by permission from *New England Review,* Vol. IV, No. 3, 1982 and Vol. VI, No. 3, 1983, Copyright by Stephen Dunn; *The New Yorker:* "Nova Scotia," Reprinted by permission, originally in *The New Yorker,* Copyright 1983 by Stephen Dunn; *The Ohio Review:* "Whiteness," "The Routine Things Around The House"; *Poetry:* "Corners," "Eggs," "The End," "In The Blowdown Zone," "The Snow Leopard," "Elegy"; *Poetry Northwest:* "In The 20th Century," "Wavelengths," "Climbing Ladders Anyway," "The Wild"; *The Poetry Review:* "Being Fair With Numbers," Reprinted by permission of the Poetry Society of America, originally published in *The Poetry Review,* Vol. 1, No. 1, Copyright 1983 by Stephen Dunn; *Tar River Poetry:* "Solar Eclipse," "Laws," "An American Film"; *The Virginia Quarterly Review:* "The Landscape"; *The Yale Review:* "Tangier"

Many thanks to The National Endowment for the Arts, Stockton State College, and to Yaddo for their support and aid.

Special thanks to Donald Lawder, Lawrence Raab and Ellen Bryant Voigt for their criticism and suggestions.

The publication of this book is supported by grants from the National Endowment for the Arts in Washington, D. C., a Federal agency, and from the Pennsylvania Council on the Arts. Books in the Carnegie-Mellon University Press Poetry Series are distributed by the University of Pittsburgh Press, 127 N. Bellefield Avenue, Pittsburgh, Pennsylvania 15260

Library of Congress Catalog Card Number 84-70175
ISBN 0-88748-000-4
ISBN 0-88748-001-2
Copyright © 1984 by Stephen Dunn
Printed and bound in the United States of America
First Edition

For Lois

CONTENTS

I.

II.

III.

I

CORNERS

I've sought out corner bars, lived in corner houses;
    like everyone else I've reserved
corner tables, thinking they'd be sufficient.
    I've met at corners
perceived as crossroads, loved to find love
    leaning against a lamp post
but have known the abruptness of corners too,
    the pivot, the silence.
I've sat in corners at parties hoping for someone
    who knew the virtue
of both distance and close quarters, someone with a
    corner person's taste
for intimacy, hard won, rising out of shyness
    and desire.
And I've turned corners there was no going back to,
    corners
in the middle of a room that led
    to Spain or solitude.
And always the thin line between corner
    and cornered,
the good corners of bodies and those severe bodies
    that permit no repose,
the places we retreat to, the places we can't bear
    to be found.

BLUES FOR ANOTHER TIME

Once again, darkness. Moments before
swallows making designs in the sky.
Now all that's delicate has made friends
with something strong, or has gone underground or home.
A Billie Holiday song coming
from the new neighbor's house.
Friends there, perhaps.
Yet it seems to have begun again,
the old original condition,
an overrated moon up above
and the dark so palpable
I could mistake color for density,
reach up and try to hold on.
A dog nearby doesn't understand his chain.
He and Billie Holiday singing along.
Once, I suppose, the world was clear.
Fear was pure as hunger itself
and no animal slept with its belly up.
Tonight I want the obvious wound
and the inexhaustible explanation of it
to exist side by side.
I want both stitches and salve.
I knew twins who hated each other,
but wore matching clothes.
That's the way things are, I know.
That's as clear as they're likely to get.
Love me, love me not.
All one can do is sing about that.

THE END

The vandals stole the street signs
   and in a sense, unnamed,
      we didn't live anywhere,

the house numbers began to float,
   visitors after dark were told
      there'd be a light on,

that if they got lost
   there was a phone nearby
      but exactly where we couldn't say —

everywhere the signs were gone.
   The postman arrived by memory
      but when the vandals

took our names off the mailbox
   in a sense we didn't exist
      or if we existed

were interchangeable:
   I got Harrison's divorce papers,
      he got rejected poems.

One day we saw the mail truck
   circling the neighborhood
      like a lost dog, and

it got worse. Night after night
   the same lewd, insidious moan
      forced us

to take the phone off the hook.
   Busy, busy, busy —
      said all our friends.

We put the receiver back
   but soon no one called
      except him or her or they

so we took to moaning in response
   without humor or passion,
      happy in a sense

to have made some connection.
   Deep down it satisfied no one.
      Soon it was over, done with.

SOLAR ECLIPSE

Nova Scotia, 1972

Birds that never had flown in the dark
   circled wildly, confused.

And there were unexpected stars as the moon
   slid across.

The light returned in slivers, everything was
   moving, even speech

sought to collide with the blur
   the heart makes

out of fact, and speech failed.
   Everything got calm.

The blue heron returned to the double
   morning of the day.

The birds caucussed in the trees.
   At a time like this

someone trembling must have spoken
   the first prayer.

What more to say except the miraculous world
   didn't change.

The moon that night was just the moon,
   deadpan, its afternoon kiss

in the cool past.

IN THE BLOWDOWN ZONE

Mount St. Helens,
  one year after

The fireweed, the Canada thistle, the bracken fern
  send up their stems
    through the crust of ash,

come from underneath like great, forgotten ideas.
  This is spring at its best,
    shrugging off death

in the blowdown zone, in the land
  of "the standing dead."
    Some raccoons return,

some porcupines. It will take one hundred years
  for things to be right.
    We'll have to wait, we who

will die waiting, thinking only of ourselves.
  In the meantime we repeat
    this broken syllogism

like a prayer: There's no nitrogen in ash.
  No plant can live without nitrogen.
    The fireweed is coming up.

BEING FAIR WITH NUMBERS

I take the number eleven and pull it apart.
Now there's one for me, one for you.
This is called being fair with numbers.

I could've chosen ten, but zero
is nothing to give anyone, and one then
would've become too important

like an obelisk in an empty room.
Be careful not to add your one
to another one, at least not for a while.

Yours is an eleven at heart,
not something on its way to being two,
not that bourgeois. It's sad, though,

this preoccupation with being fair.
One alone is one alone, no matter
how it got that way, or what it once was.

But who knows what's happy?
It was, as always, a question
of the greater good. An honorable man

doesn't keep an eleven for himself.
There are nightrides, there are revolutions
for less than that.

ATLANTIC CITY

To stare at the ocean in winter
  is to know
    the variety in repetition.

It's to understand repetition's secret
  link with solace.
    How often I went to it, lonely,

wanting its sexual music, its applause.
  How often it took my mood
    and deepened it, instructed me

loneliness is nothing special,
  that I was anybody, a man.
    Yesterday at the blackjack table,

a few hundred yards from the shore,
  I doubled-down with eleven
    and drew a three. That was it.

I walked up North Carolina to Arctic
  all alone. The wind suggested
    wonderful movement at sea.

I didn't care. I didn't care if
  the waves were high and white
    or if the seagulls

were dropping clam shells from the sky.
  I had a loser's thought: how wise I was
    for not paying to park.

That's what I said to myself
  far away from myself
    with the ocean now two blocks away;

how wise I was. The houses started to speak
of ruin. Boards on some windows.
Wine bottles in doorways.

To stare at a city half in ruin,
half in glitter,
is to know why the beach

and its beautiful desolation in winter
is a fearsone place
if one risks being calm and clear.

I wish I could say I turned around.

RESPONSE TO A LETTER FROM FRANCE

"We're living in a Socialist paradise.
My mind boggles when I think where
you live."

All the trees are in bloom
though the gypsy moths, with their plague
mentality, are blossoming too.
Don't feel sorry for us. We've even learned
to live amid Republicans; the avarice
of gypsy moths is only a little more
mindless, effective. It's okay here.
The ocean isn't perfectly clean
but on good days when I get low enough
the waves push me out ahead of them;
lacking wings or an engine
it's the closest thing to flight.
In France, where life and theory
touch now and then,
I don't doubt your pleasures. But here
there's room enough for incorrect
behavior, which some of us plan on.
There are casinos and fifty or sixty miles
of pines to get lost in.
Socialism makes good sense, sure.
But we actually have four people
who love us, the tennis courts aren't
crowded, our neighbor who has no politics
was generous yesterday for other reasons.
At another time I would offer you
what falls short of promise, the America
outside of me and my part in it.
But not when you feel sorry for us.
I just killed a Brown Recluse spider.
The sun is out. I want you to know
the afternoon is ablaze with ordinary people,
smiling, full of hidden unfulfillment,
everywhere, my friend, everywhere.

South Jersey
July 15, 1981

20

THE LANDSCAPE

For Lois

Flood waters in Brigantine.
   And the ocean: a shark
      for every pearl.

So we did the safe thing,
   a house eight miles in
      on the edge of the Barrens,

no pure sand, but the soil
   that has sand in it
      in which scrub oaks grow.

We should have known nothing's safe.
   That love is an ocean too.
      That locks break if touched

just right. And so we live now
   with the doors open, the heart
      learning about the fullness and ache

that comes from letting in.
   The flowers are rose and violet.
      They grow in spite

of where we live. Three miles away
   the old vegetable man thinks
      now of drought, now of rain.

We try to buy from him.
   We try to do the right thing
      but sometimes we lick the palm

of a middleman, change the balance,
    follow our hungers.
        Everyone suffers.

This landscape won't stop.
    This landscape is everywhere.
        Come fall we find ourselves

on our knees, doing what must be done
    in the yard. The cold comes.
        The cold is wisdom

saying huddle together, go inside.
    And the cold follows us
        as far as it can.

IN THE 20TH CENTURY

Someone left green plastic bags full of leaves
    amid fallen leaves at the edge
        of the forest

and there they remained all fall
    like bad modern art,
        like a statement

half thought out, or fully thought out
    by someone half capable
        of thought.

I'd pass them on the road to work
    and would continue on
        in the vague way

most of us continue on, thinking of the
    previous night's quarrel or how
        the sun visor, tilted down,

allowed me to see ahead just enough.
    I was tempted to slit the bags
        open, and once

I dwelt on what this might mean
    to the wilderness, but even then
        I smiled.

It was, I suppose, the smile that accepts
    everything and nothing, the smile
        each of us saves

if not to save ourselves, then to save
    the situation. It's spring now
        near the end

of the century, a natural green mingles
with what looks like
strange bushes, mutants

from some unaccountable marriage —
as if a man, lonely enough
to figure a way,

had gone too far with an experiment.

THE DINNER

At dinner, because our hosts had been
   quarreling and couldn't hide it,
      we felt the old need

to charm, to literally enchant
   which also means subdue,
      and they allowed us

to charm them with stories from our day
   which had been full
      of small affections

and a separateness — *a bringing from* —
   and so meant closeness.
      They were kind to allow us

to charm them, feeling as they were
   those ember-like resentments,
      subterranean,

that come from unfinished quarrels.
   But finally charm wasn't equal
      to what they were feeling

and words slipped out, *tones*, then
   the terrible polite talk
      of pass this, pass that, thank you.

One year earlier we were them and knew
   what it would be like after
      we left, how evenings

like this end in separate rooms
or with violent, not quite
cathartic lovemaking.

We said goodbye as soon as we could,
leaving them to what must be
played out, essential as breathing.

In the car we talked about it,
not without pleasure.
There was a low fog

and as we drove it parted, and kept
parting (What else could it do?)
all the way home.

ALMOST EVERYONE

For Milan Kundera

There are borders toward which
everyone is moving, he thought —
a living room perhaps
where two people begin to float

in the air outside their own lives,
their words empty suitcases
punctuated by travel stickers . . .
a border reached after years

of slippage and sleep.
To invent the future, then,
is to reduce the hazards of being
extinguished by it, he thought,

and conjured a black rainbow
arched over a city,
a giant screen below
on which lovers could be seen

making love. But no matter
how hard he tried
he couldn't help but invent the present,
burdened as he was

by his participation in it,
his desperate hopefulness.
Black rainbows, making love under them . . .
how common!

Yet who could live in the present
with its constant cancellations,
its borders that looked like paths?
Almost everyone, he decided.

SICK DAYS

On this street where the red flag
on the mailbox signals someone
has thought of me, and an empty box
means more to me than it should,

I envy only one of my neighbors
and despise two of them, and the woman
I think I could like flirts too much
with anyone who knocks.

The junkman down the block
searched my garbage today,
shook his head, and moved on.
The newspaper boy: another errant toss.

No one should stay at home.
To stay home is to believe too much
in the cycle of the water pump,
the ritual of cleanliness and food.

It is to risk only small failures,
to lose touch with home
as a refuge, a place to return to,
that animal wisdom of the cave.

Here, looking out the window, sick
with a common sickness,
I want my neighbors to be there
only when I need them;

the one with the pick-up —
a friend when the leaves fall.
Anyone with a power saw —
let generosity be his fault.

To them I want to be known
as decent but a little strange, home
only in the evening, available
for emergencies of a very specific kind.

ELEGY

John Cheever
1912 - 1982

Those men going home on trains,
those husbands who arrive
astounded to find their wives
the same people they've always been,
have lost the man who loved them enough
to show their foolishness, and ours.
There was no complicity quite like his;
those sentences washing over us,
never sentencing.

* * *

Dirty socks on the bedroom floor.
Some flirtation at a party.
And late one night the screaming starts.
Now here comes forgiveness
in its tattered clothes.
But there's no forgiving.
It's just a word they use
at times like this.

* * *

They're drinking too much in Connecticut,
fabricating lives in Italy.
They're making love again
because nothing's on T.V.
And one man, my favorite,
with just two weeks vacation
and a gloomy brother ruining it,
lectures him on grace
and later sees his sister
and his wife, naked and unshy,
walk toward him out of the sea.

* * *

When the 5:48 comes
she has a gun and is walking behind him.
He should have known: you don't
have an affair with anyone
more needy than yourself.
And if she's your secretary
you then don't fire her.
There's a kind of justice
when she forces his face into the mud.
She's a little crazy
and he's a bastard. Not one of us
can feel wholly good.

* * *

Unfulfillment is what they're full of,
swimming neighbors' pools
or sitting in empty offices,
heroic as salmon.
During the day
the eye, on its way to sports,
passes over the obituaries
and suddenly the babysitter is an antidote
to a hundred afternoons.

* * *

The suburban mirrors have clouded some.
The privacies of marriage,
those longings for a crisis,
have many recorders
but few with balance.
Who now, among us,
will take the solemn out of serious?

ESSAY ON THE PERSONAL

Because finally the personal
is all that matters,
we spend years describing stones,
chairs, abandoned farm houses —
until we're ready. Always
it's a matter of precision,
what it feels like
to kiss someone or to walk
out the door. How good it was
to practice on stones
which were things we could love
without weeping over. How good
someone else abandoned the farm house,
bankrupt and desperate.
Now we can bring a fine edge
to our parents. We can hold hurt
up to the sun for examination.
But just when we think we have it,
the personal goes the way of
belief. What seemed so deep
begins to seem naïve, something
that could be trusted
because we hadn't read Plato
or held two contradictory ideas
or women in the same day.
Love, then, becomes an old movie.
Loss seems so common
it belongs to the air,
to breath itself, anyone's.
We're left with style, a particular
way of standing and saying,
the idiosyncratic look
at the frown which means nothing
until we say it does. Years later,

long after we believed it peculiar
to ourselves, we return to love.
We return to everything
strange, inchoate, like living
with someone, like living alone,
settling for the partial, the almost
satisfactory sense of it.

KANSAS

I've imagined a heaven
of replications, dull, pacific,
a place where you're sent
for having been a gentleman
in the face of great passion.
In short, I've imagined and lived
lesser moments than this,
fixed as it is
in its quiet passing, a house
full of plants, animals, windows,
and the faint ticking of the dishwasher
in its cycle of drying.
The spirit is asleep
in its sac of comfort.
The blood that rushes to the penis
has no reason to move.
                    Truth is
everyone knows comfort
is wonderful, even dullness
is wonderful if the heart's right,
the mind at ease with it. Truth is
there's always another person
concealed in a poem
or down the street or across the country,
but in this case she's upstairs
in her vague purgatory, that Kansas
of affections.
I didn't know I was concealing her
until this moment, which changes nothing,
the dishwasher finished now,
the windows offering a view
I've often known from the other side —
unspectacular, blameless.

THE ROOM AND THE WORLD

The room was room enough for one
or maybe two if the two had just
discovered each other and were one.
Outside of the room was the world
which had a key to the room, and knowing
a little about the world he knew
how pointless it was to change the lock.
He knew the world could enter the room
anytime it wanted, but for the present
the world was content to do its damage
elsewhere, which the television recorded.
Always, he kept in his mind the story of the man
hanging from a cliff, how the wildflowers
growing there looked lovelier than ever.
That was how he felt about his one chair
and the geometry of the hangers in his closet
and the bed that fit him like a body shirt.
Sometimes the world would breathe heavily
outside the door because it was obscene
and could not help itself. It was this
that led him eventually to love the world
for its pressure and essential sadness.
One day he just found himself opening
the door, allowing the inevitable.
The world came in and filled the room.
It seemed so familiar with everything.

AFLOAT

From the crude jetty cormorants stare
as I try to relax in deep water.
This is the mixed joy the illicit brings,
floating on my back
uselessly on a weekday
while the earth teeter-totters on its axis,
fat men on each side.
I've been trying to convince myself
living requires a certain forgetfulness.
Here's the trial by water
and I must be innocent, bobbing like this
far above the bottom.

But I can see the lush green
of the mountains where the poor on footpaths
are carrying things homeward.
Once I might have imagined a laying down
of burdens, festivals after dark.
Now, in small groups getting larger,
people are planning, not dancing.
For us afloat in the wrong waters
soon not even a nice day
with its camouflage, not even forgetfulness
will do any good.

The day is brilliant, though.
And something's ruling me
the way a mistake rules an option.
It's time to swim in.
I close my eyes, lie still.

Venezuela, 1981

35

II

THE ROUTINE THINGS AROUND
THE HOUSE

When mother died
I thought: now I'll have a death poem.
That was unforgivable

yet I've since forgiven myself
as sons are able to do
who've been loved by their mothers.

I stared into the coffin
knowing how long she'd live,
how many lifetimes there are

in the sweet revisions of memory.
It's hard to know exactly
how we ease ourselves back from sadness,

but I remembered when I was twelve,
1951, before the world
unbuttoned its blouse.

I had asked my mother (I was trembling)
if I could see her breasts
and she took me into her room

without embarrassment or coyness
and I stared at them,
afraid to ask for more.

Now, years later, someone tells me
Cancers who've never had mother love
are doomed and I, a Cancer,

feel blessed again. What luck
to have had a mother
who showed me her breasts

when girls my age were developing
their separate countries,
what luck

she didn't doom me
with too much or too little.
Had I asked to touch,

perhaps to suck them,
what would she have done?
Mother, dead woman

who I think permits me
to love women easily,
this poem

is dedicated to where
we stopped, to the incompleteness
that was sufficient

and to how you buttoned up,
began doing the routine things
around the house.

LEGACY

For my father,
Charles Dunn (1905-1967)

1.

The Photograph

My father is in Captain Starns,
a restaurant in Atlantic City.
It's 1950,
I'm there too, eleven years old.
He sold more Frigidaires

than anyone. That's why we're there,
everything free.
It's before the house started
to whisper, before testimony
was called for and lives got ruined.

My father is smiling. I'm smiling.
There's a bowl of shrimp
in front of us.
We have identical shirts on,
short sleeve with little sailboats.
It's before a difference set in

between corniness and happiness.
Soon I'll get up
and my brother will sit next to him.
Mother will click the shutter.
We believe in fairness,

we still believe America
is a prayer, an anthem.
Though his hair is receding
my father's face says nothing
can stop him.

2.

The Secret

When Mother asked him
where the savings went, he said
"the track" and became lost
in his own house, the wastrel,
my mother and her mother
doling out money to him
the rest of his life.

I was sixteen when he told me
the truth, making me his private son,
making anger the emotion
I still have to think about.
I see now that chivalric code
held like a child's song

in the sanctum of his decency,
the error that led to error,
the eventual blur of it all.
And so many nights in the livingroom
the pages of a newspaper being turned

and his sound — scotch over ice
in a large glass — how conspicuous
he must have felt,
his best gesture gone wrong,
history changed, the days going on and on.

3.

The Family

The family I was part of
was always extended, grandfather
and grandmother on my mother's side
living with us, and grandfather
with a mistress only my father

knew about, beautiful supposedly
and poor. When she began to die
and wouldn't die fast,
when money became love's test,
grandfather had no one

to turn to except my father
who gave him everything.
It was a pact between men,
a handshake and a secret,
then the country turned

to war and all other debts
must have seemed just personal.
Every night the two of them
huddled by the radio waiting for news
of the clear, identifiable enemy.

4.

The Silence

My father became a salesman
heavy with silence.
When he spoke he was charming,
allowed everyone to enjoy
not knowing him.

Nights he'd come home drunk
mother would cook his food
and there'd be silence.
Thus, for years, I thought
all arguments were silent
and this is why silence
is what I arm myself with
and silence is what I hate.

Sleep for him was broken speech,
exclamations, the day come back.
Sleep was the surprise
he'd wake up from, on the couch,
still in his clothes.

I carry silence with me
the way others carry snapshots
of loved ones. I offer it
and wait for a response.

5.

The Visitation

At the airport, on my way to Spain,
he shook my hand too hard,
said goodbye too long.

I spent his funeral in a room
in Cadiz, too poor to fly back
and paying for what I couldn't afford.

The night he died, the night before
the telegram arrived,
something thumped all night

on the flat roof.
It was my father, I think,
come to be let in.

I was in another country,
living on savings. It must have seemed
like heaven to him.

CLIMBING LADDERS ANYWAY

The first was wooden with a missing rung.
  We kept it on three hooks
    in the garage

and when it was time for storm windows
  my father, two hundred pounds,
    would ask me to hold it

while he climbed to what seemed
  like injury, taking that big step
    where the missing rung was

and placing all his weight on the rung
  above it, which would bend.
    That was how I learned

to be afraid of ladders and to climb them
  anyway; the cold was coming,
    to stay down

wasn't one of his choices. Even today
  the aluminum ladder I own
    reaches far beyond

where I feel good about going.
  But I bought it, I knew
    the roof, maybe the sky,

would someday ask me of something simple
  and terrifying, and I wanted
    to be ready

as my father would have been
  to climb to whatever
    had to be done — as now,

having placed the ladder against the house,
    I move toward the loose antenna,
        my children watching

and me thinking nothing but the antenna,
    nothing but this specific
        and necessary adjustment.

BRIEFCASES

Fifteen years ago I found my father's
   in the family attic, so used
      the shoemaker had to
repair it, and I kept it like love

until it couldn't be kept any more.
   Then my father-in-law died
      and I got his, almost
identical, just the wrong initials

embossed in gold. It's forty years old,
   falling apart, soon
      there'll be nothing
that smells of father-love and that difficulty

of living with fathers, but I'd prefer
   a paper bag to those
      new briefcases
made for men living fast-forward

or those attaché cases that match
   your raincoat and spring open
      like a salute
and a click of heels. I'm going

to put an ad in the paper, "Wanted:
   Old briefcase, accordion style,"
      and I won't care
whose father it belonged to

if it's brown and the divider keeps
   things on their proper side.
      Like an adoption
it's sure to feel natural before long —

a son without a father, but with this
   one briefcase carrying
     a replica
comfortably into the future,

 something for an empty hand, sentimental
   the way keeping is
     sentimental, for *keep-*
sake, with clarity and without tears.

TRAVELING TO NOVA SCOTIA

We take the Bluenose
out of Bar Harbor,
choppy seas, the girls
riding the wave

between nausea and excitement.
They're nine and twelve,
their mother home, working,
all the rules now

uncertain, negotiable
up to a point. In truth,
I'm the autocrat
with the democratic pose —

every decision
an illusion of consensus.
Soon the passage
into other waters,

the learning to live
with two lives
set in motion years ago,
already charted.

This ship, going forward
in fog, is made for this rocking
and worse. The girls are
full of disaster movies —

when the foghorn sounds
they think *iceberg, lifeboat.*
They think all accidents
are large. If I have a job

it's to offer the alternative
truths. It's to insist
we keep going
and then we arrive.

Of course I say nothing
so direct. I put my arms
around them. When we don't die
it's a small triumph

for this kind of loving,
another stay
against what's out there,
what they suspected all along.

III

LAWS

A black cat wanders out into
an open field. How vulnerable it is,
how even its own shadow
causes it to stop and hunch.
Mice come, hundreds of them,
forming a circle around the cat.
They've been waiting for months
to catch the cat like this.
But the cat is suddenly unafraid.
Though the mice have their plans,
have worked on tactics and tricks,
none of them moves.
The cat thinks: all I have to do
is be who I am. And it's right.
One quick move
and the mice scatter, go home.

After humiliation, home is a hole
where no one speaks. Mouse things
get done, and then there is
the impossibility of sleep.
They curse nature, they curse
their small legs and hearts.
We all know stories of how, after
great defeat, the powerless rise up.
But not if they're mice.
The cat waits for them in the tall grass.
The mice are constantly surprised.

EGGS

I never used to like eggs, that conspicuous
    breaking and ooze like a cow
being slaughtered in the kitchen
    before the steak is served.

And my father wanting his sunny-side-up
    which seemed wrong,
like exposing yourself. But I loved to look
    at unbroken eggs, I loved

to hold them in my hand and toss them up,
    always feeling I knew
how high was too high, always
    coming away clean.

Years later, I'd discover, through Blake,
    you can't get away clean.
You have to know what's more than enough
    to know what's enough,

the game I played was á coward's game.
    I liked my eggs hard boiled
at first, then deviled, ice cold.
    Scrambled was years off;

breaking and cooking them myself — more years.
    One Halloween I stole eggs
from the egg farm, extra large, to throw at girls.
    Loving the shape of eggs,

confused by the shape of girls, I loved
    to see the egg break
on their jeans, loved the screams and the stain.
    Now I suck eggs

after making a little hole in the tip.
  I've made peace with the yolk.
I no longer think of the whites as coming
  face to face with the blind.

I almost can forget how the conglomerates
  have made chickens slaves,
the small cages and the perpetual light.
  I love eggs now,

I love women; I keep eggs to myself.
  As for the chicken and the egg
I say the egg was first. The egg is perfect.
  It always was.

The chicken, like most children, an afterthought.

THE SNOW LEOPARD

After seeing the magnificent blue sheep
high in the Himalayas
Matthiessen wondered if he'd seen enough,
if seeing the snow leopard
wouldn't bring "the desolation of success."
Down here, where we live,
there's just this visible world
and the other world inside it,
the rag lady of Bank Street
sitting with her look-alike dog
and somewhere something else
like the dark rosettes hidden beneath
the fur of the snow leopard.
We buy food at the grocery store,
scotch enough to last
an ordinary week.
We break down in private,
screaming for love.
Always, up there, there's a Matthiessen
trekking through snow to the top
of something, finding peace
with difficulty, then losing it.
He never saw the snow leopard;
he knew it saw him.
Every day the words "too little"
and "too much" visit each other,
get mixed up.
The boy with orange hair
zips his leather jacket as we pass.
A girl on rollerskates
is half rockette, half American flag.
We're at sea level, and once
from out of the sea came something like us
as now, climbing steps to our apartment,
we rise higher and higher —
then the unsatisfactory,
the successful key in the lock.

DESIRE

I remember how it used to be
at noon, springtime, the city streets
full of office workers like myself
let loose from the cold
glass buildings on Park and Lex,
the dull swaddling of winter cast off,
almost everyone wanting
everyone else. It was amazing
how most of us contained ourselves,
bringing desire back up
to the office where it existed anyway,
quiet, like a good engine.
I'd linger a bit
with the receptionist,
knock on someone else's open door,
ease myself, by increments,
into the seriousness they paid me for.
Desire was everywhere those years,
so enormous it couldn't be reduced
one person at a time.
I don't remember when it was,
though closer to now than then,
I walked the streets desireless,
my eyes fixed on destination alone.
The beautiful person across from me
on the bus or train
looked like effort, work.
I translated her into pain.
For months I had the clarity
the cynical survive with,
their world so safely small.
Today, walking 57th toward 3rd,
it's all come back,
the interesting, the various,
the conjured life suggested by a glance.
I praise how the body heals itself.
I praise how, finally, it never learns.

CHOOSING TO THINK OF IT

Today, ten thousand people will die
and their small replacements will bring joy
and this will make sense to someone
removed from any sense of loss.
I, too, will die a little and carry on,
doing some paperwork, driving myself
home. The sky is simply overcast,
nothing is less than it was
yesterday and the day before. In short,
there's no reason or every reason
why I'm choosing to think of this now.
The short-lived holiness
true lovers know, making them unaccountable
except to spirit and themselves — suddenly
I want to be that insufferable and selfish,
that sharpened and tuned.
I'm going to think of what it means
to be an animal crossing a highway,
to be a human without a useful prayer
setting off on one of those journeys
we humans take. I don't expect anything
to change. I just want to be filled up
a little more with what exists,
tipped toward the laughter which understands
I'm nothing and all there is.
By evening the promised storm will arrive.
A few in small boats will be taken by surprise.
There will be survivors, and even they will die.

IN DEFENSE OF BLOWFISH

"There's always some poison in blowfish,
how much the eater doesn't know."

In Japan, where blowfish is a delicacy,
a little death must equal a little pleasure —
like deciding to kiss
a woman you've just met, the handle
of a knife protruding from her boot —
or the taste must be so good
you simply can't resist.
Four or five Japanese die each year
from blowfish, the reports say.
But whole families dine on it,
and a good restaurant controls the poison
so that the eater feels
only a slight numbness around the lips.
Imagine how fine the conversation must be!
Imagine, when the effect sets in,
the immense feeling of love for one another,
how whatever could be slipping away
must be spoken and held.

AN AMERICAN FILM

A rainbow appeared with its promises,
its lore. At a moment like this, I thought,
something might begin for someone else.

The grass was wet. The air chlorophyll.
I walked across the grass
as if I were watching myself

walk across the grass. There was no romance
to the way she waited at the curb
next to the Mazda. She, in fact, was impatient

and I apologized for the lateness
of the hour, the absence
of something graceful, redemptive.

I said, "Look at the rainbow,"
but felt foolish
as if I had said something in song.

Elsewhere things were probably beginning
for other people; kisses, ideas.
We got in the car and drove to Brazil.

No, we got in the car and began
the speaking parts from the life we were in,
then drove to the party.

The sky was a blue helmet
worn by a large invisible clown.
The party was barbecue, backyard.

I knew a good story about a green-head fly
and moved from person to person
telling it. I told it with charm,

hearing myself tell it,
knowing how insignificant it was —
a chance to exhibit pure style.

The woman I arrived with smiled
from across the yard. I felt I should
caress her cheek, take her aside.

Perhaps someone who believed rainbows
were for him, was boarding a plane now
ignorant of the story he was in

as only major characters can be.
The hot dogs smelled like good memories.
The bean salad glistened

on its white tray. It was still afternoon,
still only the middle of what
was not much different

from what it felt like, or seemed.

NOVA SCOTIA

Jelly fish washed up
like small blue parachutes
but it was the silent fishing of cranes
that signalled another time
had begun, another world.
I walked to the clam bed
with bucket and pitchfork
and before the sun had fallen
we had steamers
and Black Point darkened
slowly, layer upon layer.
The temperature dropped
into the fifties; how easily we fell
into that smug summer sleep
of people vacationing in the north.

One July, though, out of love
with each other,
we played frisbee, perfecting
the sidearm, the between-the-legs.
In bed we did it this way,
then that, sad masters of technique.
Then a crane dragged
its damaged leg into the tall reeds,
snapped and hissed
when we got near, would not
let itself be saved.
In the morning
we found its neck ripped —
a weasel's work, pure mischief,
and we felt, no, we were sure
nothing we did or didn't do
could have changed a thing.

TANGIER

There's no salvation in elsewhere;
forget the horizon, the seductive sky.
If nothing's here, nothing's there.

I know. Once I escaped to Tangier,
took the same face, the same lie.
There's no salvation in elsewhere

when elsewhere has empty rooms, mirrors.
Everywhere: the capital I.
If nothing's here, nothing's there

unless, of course, your motive's secure;
not therapy, but joy,
salvation an idea left behind, elsewhere,

like overweight baggage or yesteryear.
The fundamental things apply.
If nothing's here, nothing's there —

I brought with me my own imperfect air.
The streets were noise. The heart dry.
There was no salvation elsewhere.
I came with nothing, found nothing there.

FIXED

The Cascades to the northeast, Ranier
   on a clear day
      as haunting as a dare —

I hate how after a while I learn
   to live with such things, beauty
      the stunning girl next door

with the dull inner life, her boyfriends
   with all those muscles
      in their legs.

Time to move on,
   or to look down the street
      at the street, candy wrappers

and stray pennies, a torn note perhaps,
   a piece of somebody's
      less than perfect life.

Where I come from all that's interesting
   has to be imagined, a mountain
      with a fire escape,

women coming out of trees.
   If Stevens is right the imagination
      is just a lamp, changes nothing.

Still I'd like to change something
   if I could do it brilliantly,
      if the mountains here

were not so fixed in their grandeur.
   In Atlantic City where the dismal
      avenues invite the reds and yellows,

the splashes of my best self,
  I've found myself smiling, capable
    of some great transformational love

as I've walked past the slums
  and slick hotels. I've forced myself
    to see a nude descending

a staircase in the heart of the city,
  the passers-by startled coming together
    to form an audience

that moments before
  were men and women with tired eyes
    looking for bargains.

Seattle, 1980

ENOUGH TIME

For Lyn Harrison

I used to think:
out of small things, a lifetime.
Out of a night full of stars,
a universe. But tonight
I want to pick, deny,
believe only in the irrational
pull upwards
to where the gods lie
in their spacious graves.
Out of small things, perhaps,
fragments, a scattering.
Out of a night full of stars,
one that falls
seemingly in our direction.
Enough. All that's falling
is the temperature. And the world
is down here in neighborhoods
where the trash piles up
and I've danced
and, in time, will dance again.
I know the moon, this awful night,
is saying something
uplifting to the sea.
I know starfish and sharks
exist without contradiction.
        Lyn dead at thirty-one
who allowed me to compliment her
on her thinness when only she knew.
Lyn, who had enough time
to be appalled and fascinated.

WHITENESS

On the way to Cottonwood, Minnesota,
along Route 23,
a white horse used to graze —
apparitional, always startling —
like birches suddenly among evergreens.
Eight years have passed
and it's become something clean
and unharnessed for the mind to hold
amid the rush of atrocities;
I see it lifting
its head, cantering toward a barn
where no other animal lived.
There are friends I could ask
but I don't want to know if the horse
is still there or how the winters
might have changed it.
Here there are billboards
on the marshland where egrets
once lived, and that's enough of progress,
enough of the way of things.
Years ago, before experience,
I watched a lovely woman
walk toward me naked,
carrying her shyness like a gift,
and that woman and that horse
are among the photographs untaken
that I plan to die with,
vivid in their whiteness,
pumping blood to and from the heart
even after, maybe for a second or two,
my eyes close and there's nothing.

SILENCE

I've heard people at campgrounds
with their portable radios all the way up,
and I've found them in restaurants,
their public voices rattling the spoons,
and I've sat through that different
more silent noise
of those who are too serious
or not serious enough

but right now it's my own porch,
night almost here in my own world,
and I don't want to listen to boys playing war
and the dogs barking
and my neighbor, the wife-beater,
closing his shed.
My child whose knee has been bruised
needs to be calmed

and I'd like to give her a perfect
kind of quiet, with whispers and balm
in it, then I want her to go away,
let the night arrive
as it might have arrived
a hundred thousand years ago, the moon
taking on definition in the sky
and all the creatures that exist
looking up, amazed.

MIDDLE CLASS POEM

In dreams, the news of the world
comes back, gets mixed up
with our parents and the moon.
We can't help but thrash.
Those with whom we sleep, never equally,
roll away from us and sigh.

When we wake
the news of the world embraces us,
pulls back. Who let go first? —
a lover's question, the lover
who's most alone.
We purchase a little forgetfulness
at the mall. We block the entrance
to our hearts.

Come evening, the news of the world
is roaming the streets
while we bathe our children,
while we eat what's plentiful
and scarce. We know what we need
to keep out, what's always there —
painful to look at, bottomless.

AN ARGUMENT WITH WISDOM
AT MONTAUK

We've just two days, Zen time:
if we don't try to fill them
they might be full.

But we were born in the east,
not in the East.
What can we do?

There are cliffs to climb.
There's an old lighthouse at the Point.
And here at the motel

the untanned parts of us
are neon signs saying *Here.*
It's not reality we're after,

it's preferences.
We go toward things
vagrant as the gulls,

elevated and reduced
by appetite,
always in transit.

I touch you.
I wish for the days
to be measured by touch,

to find time
for the lighthouse too.
If I had a choice, this is how

the universe would be understood:
bodies in motion. The astronomy
of the small lamp by the bed.

WAVELENGTHS

1

It's the role of objects like the table,
or the vase, to restore silence
to a room where a party has been.
They do it naturally when everyone's gone.
It's a kind of keeping, a breathing in.

2

Not the nipple, which often begs,
but where the breast first seems to rise,
that arc above the rib cage.
To follow that arc to the nipple
is the tongue's quiet way home,
its lovely path through the snow.

3

I opened the back windows in the dark
and made mouse sounds
so the owl would come.
When I shone the light on the trees
there it was: the harsh, wide-eyed
silence of the deceived.

4

The sound an earthworm makes
is the sound of a person
moistening his lips. To hear it
you have to get beneath repulsion,
not above it. You have to love
where your lover loves your face to be.

5

Death has a sound so continuous
only the dying can differentiate it
from the absence of wind.
It's a music, my grandmother said,
both popular and private.
You'd dance to it if you could.

6

We, who've had experience with the dark
and know how it speaks,
keep the nightlight on, postpone lying down.
A night will come when my daughter, too,
won't sleep. But now from her room
the steady hum of good news.

7

At the center of a stone is more stone.
To find a heart, even a hard one,
when a heart is of no use
is bad poetry, like saying home is sweet.
Put a stone to your ear.
How it mocks what you want to hear.

8

If there's a sound to starlight
it exists the way a gesture
exists to more than the eye.
Meaningless, unless you love the star,
it could be the sound of dust
being touched by sun in a vacant room.

9

The unspoken sits down with us again.
We know it by the way it speaks
of other things, by our need to scream.
Each of us thinks the other has invited it.
Neither of us will send it away.
It drinks our wine. It whispers in bed.

10

To ants there must be a cosmology of dirt.
Dirt, food, that's all there is.
Everytime we step on a mound, or scatter it,
we alter a universe. Oh, bastards
are part of life. It goes without saying
in the corridors of the dirt.

THE WILD

It's October. The cold again.
Both sides of the world
are deadly now to the wasp
walking on my side.
I've opened the window, preferring
to have nothing to do
with even so small a death.
But the wasp won't go,
keeps walking on the clear glass.
Once when the tumor
in my dog's stomach (the dog
we thought was fat)
had grown too large, he disappeared
and I found him on the edge
of the woods, near the cage
of a Malamute he hated.
He'd gone to die next to
something wild, in the wild.
I've always regretted
bringing him back,
my stupid human hanging-on,
that trip to the vet.
I want that wasp to die out there
where the cold hits it
like ether, and it's done.
The heat's on. The window
must feel like summer.
I suppose wasps weren't meant
to have choices or, like us,
make the short-range choice
their bodies want.
But I remember being lost
in a blizzard, the car dead,
twenty-below. The more I froze
the more I wanted to sleep,

the more my body said, lie down.
When that farmhouse appeared
(now I know what I want to say)
something beyond choice
got me there.
I want that wasp out in the air
obeying whatever it is
the species obeys when winter comes;
when it can't, but does, live on.

Carnegie-Mellon Poetry

1975
The Living and the Dead, Ann Hayes
In the Face of Descent, T. Alan Broughton

1976
The Week the Dirigible Came, Jay Meek
Full of Lust and Good Usage, Stephen Dunn

1977
How I Escaped from the Labyrinth and Other Poems,
    Philip Dacey
The Lady from the Dark Green Hills, Jim Hall
For Luck: Poems 1962-1977, H. L. Van Brunt
By the Wreckmaster's Cottage, Paula Rankin

1978
New and Selected Poems, James Bertolino
The Sun Fetcher, Michael Dennis Browne
A Circus of Needs, Stephen Dunn
The Crowd Inside, Elizabeth Libbey

1979
Paying Back the Sea, Philip Dow
Swimmer in the Rain, Robert Wallace
Far From Home, T. Alan Broughton
The Room Where Summer Ends, Peter Cooley
No Ordinary World, Mekeel McBride

1980
*And the Man Who Was Traveling Never Got
    Home,* H. L. Van Brunt
Drawing on the Walls, Jay Meek
The Yellow House on the Corner, Rita Dove
The 8-Step Grapevine, Dara Wier
The Mating Reflex, Jim Hall

1981

A Little Faith, John Skoyles
Augers, Paula Rankin
Walking Home from the Icehouse, Vern Rutsala
Work and Love, Stephen Dunn
The Rote Walker, Mark Jarman
Morocco Journal, Richard Harteis
Songs of a Returning Soul, Elizabeth Libbey

1982

The Granary, Kim R. Stafford
Calling the Dead, C. G. Hanzlicek
Dreams Before Sleep, T. Alan Broughton
Sorting it Out, Anne S. Perlman
Love Is Not a Consolation; It Is a Light, Primus St. John

1983

The Going Under of the Evening Land, Mekeel McBride
Museum, Rita Dove
Air and Salt, Eve Shelnutt
Nightseasons, Peter Cooley

1984

Falling From Stardom, Jonathan Holden
Miracle Mile, Ed Ochester
Girlfriends and Wives, Robert Wallace
Earthly Purposes Jay Meek